Words By The Wood Carver's Hands: Stories From The Brighter Side of The Woodshed

Jack Marino

Published by Ink&Chisel, 2021.

While every precaution has been taken in the preparation of this book, the publisher assumes no responsibility for errors or omissions, or for damages resulting from the use of the information contained herein.

WORDS BY THE WOOD CARVER'S HANDS: STORIES FROM THE BRIGHTER SIDE OF THE WOODSHED

First edition. February 1, 2021.

ISBN: 979-8201726546

Written by Jack Marino.

Table of Contents

To my wife, Suzanne who's love and dedication has never wavered.

To my mother Jacquelyn who kept me steady during challenging periods early in my life. You are missed very much.

Author's Prayer

I PRAY THAT EVEY ONE find the strength to dance when they feel they are about to fall. May you and your family grow like eternal gardens: strong, healthy, enduring, full of life and bursting with color. May all of you experience truck loads of patience in trying times, safe harbor in rough seas and protecting angels when the odds seem insurmountable. May your tears turn to laughter and your frowns to smiles. May you always dare to dream big with the endless possibilities of a child regardless of your age.

Acknowledgements

FIRST TO SUZANNE, JACKIE & Chet, Chris, Jeffery Ann and Lisa Ann for your input and support. This modest effort would have been monumental without you. To my high school English teacher , Ms. Claire S. at Alfred Bonnabel High School in Metairie, Louisiana (Class of 1977); your faith in me as a writer wasn't completely lost. I'm just 46 years behind on my first book. Finally to all the wood carvers and craftsmen for sharing their knowledge in trades magazines, thank you.

Beginnings

WRITING HAS ALWAYS been a part of my life. In my senior year of high school I won first place in the school's literary contest in the category of Informal essay. It is the only award I have ever won for writing. I've written poetry (sometimes as ghost writer for others), a few short stories, written letters from the heart and kept journals. Though a few attempts were made with other works, I have never been published. Now retired, one of my goals was to see to fruition, my first book.

For the most part, I never had a clear image of what the final result would look like. My only standard was that it had to convey an overall positive message. I simply wrote from the heart using accurate personal experiences to either introduce or highlight a particular message. This is where the blank page is much like the blocks of wood I use to carve an image. It is common for me to start off with one idea only to get a different result.

I've learned that creativity cannot always be forced or held to a rigid set of standards as to hinder it. Sometimes it was best to let my mind take me on a journey, destination unknown. Just enjoy the ride and see where I end up.

My interest in wood carving occurred about 12 years ago. After reading and practicing some of the carving techniques of craftsmen in trade magazines, I was instantly hooked. I have carved well over 200 pieces since then. About 75% of what I carved have been for others; annual Christmas ornaments, toys for the grandchildren, special requests from my wife and friends. The other 25% came from inspiration and simply because I have fun doing it. Initially, there was no special meaning assigned to each piece. They did seem to bring some joy to others and that was good enough for me. In time that all began to change.

Stories, eventually, began to evolve. I now believe they were there all along as they came so easily. Collectively, they spoke to me about the many blessings in my life that, perhaps, I have overlooked too often. Since stepping away from a long career, I now have a lot of time to reflect.

The stories also come from a lost tradition of story telling within my own family. The stories usually came about at those big Italian family gatherings. You knew it was story time when a family member would loudly get everyone's attention with, "Hey, remember that time when…" From there those narratives took on a life of their own with everyone adding their own colorful twist. By the time the key actors had their say, the results amounted to "Big Fish" stories. And trust me, we heard some real whoppers. The best part was that no matter the tone at the beginning, there was laughter at the end.

Part One

A Celebration of Motherhood By a Son and Husband

1. THE SOLITARY DANCER
    2. The Eternal Gardener
    3. Refilling The Nest

The Solitary Dancer

In Memory of My Mother Jacquelyn 1933-2008

Figurine Carved For The Solitary Dancer

She dances in silence as her three youngest children nap in another room forgetting, for a brief time, the hardships of her life: An orphan at age 13, a bride at 17 and now a dedicated mother of six.

Slowly, her body carries her about with grace. She is still young and beautiful with no traces of her difficult life present on her being. My mother is unaware that I watch from my bedroom doorway as she glides across the floor, eyes closed, in rhythm to the music.

She is at peace and she is calm. Her daily life is not such.

She dances for release. She dances to survive. She dances out of the love for her children.

The music will end this day and her dancing will take pause. My mother will repeat her peaceful ritual many times for the remainder of her life, this graceful, loving

Solitary Dancer.

The Eternal Gardener

Carved In Honor of My Wife, Suzanne

"Then the Lord God planted a garden in Eden..(Genesis 2:8). Then he took man and placed him in garden to cultivate and care for it (Genesis2:15)."

THROUGHOUT OUR MARRIAGE my wife has been a gardener. It was a term I neve thought much about. It all seemed so simple, find a patch of earth, dig a hole, drop the seed in, cover it with dirt, water and wait for the magic to happen. Tools were small and plant food came in canisters small enough to fit in the kitchen cabinet. She made it look all so easy. I was unaware of all the planning and preparation that was put into it, especially when the gardens were small.

And, although I benefited from the outcome, I had very little interest in the process.

As her gardens grew in scale material came in 30 pound bags and tools were much larger. This is where I became involved. My job was simply to do the heavy lifting. Or so, I thought. As I watched, she began to survey a patch of barren ground, her eyes began to shift up and down then side-to-side measuring, sectioning, planning each detail. This was the real heavy lifting.

Lowering herself to her knees, she began to instruct me where to pour the garden soil and fertilizer. Next came the mixing, the digging, the planting, the waiting then finally the daily caring. In time the seeds gave way to sprouts, then sprouts to strong stems and with plentiful leaves.

Daily she was vigilant in the garden's care, gently inspecting for diseases, protecting her seedlings from damaging invaders and unpredictable outside influences. When the stems and leaves began to turn an odd color, indicating signs of illness, she instinctively knew the appropriate treatment to restore it back to health. Because of her steady care, her seedlings grew into strong enduring stalks of beauty.

On a much more important scale, at least for this story, the skill of the gardener has been carried on in her role as a mother.

Her true flowers are her children who are now good parents themselves. This is also her gift to her grandchildren with flowers blooming into eternity.

Refilling The Nest

REPLICA OF MY SCHNAUZER, Ms. Snickers done by the author

Pets have been apart of my relationship with my wife from the very beginning. It began with her very protective black Labrador, Duke. The first time she invited me to her house (after numerous dates for breakfast in the first couple of months), Duke would not let me get out of the car to knock on the door. Hearing the commotion, she came to my rescue. In the months to come, Duke included me in his circle of protection which also included Suzanne's three children. In his canine mind I was a member of the family. Sadly, a few months before we got married, I accepted a job in Missouri. We were not allowed to have pets in the house we were going to rent so Duke was put up for adoption. Some family got themselves a great dog as both he and us started new chapters in our lives. When the oldest child graduated from high school and left for college in Mississippi, my wife went puppy shopping. By then we had moved to an apartment complex where pets were allowed. After months of looking, we welcomed an eight-week old chocolate cocker spaniel to our family. We decided to name her Cocoa and proceeded to spoil her. About once a month she was sent to the groomer to get prettied up. She was a loyal faithful companion until her passing after moving back south and settling in Mississippi. As the second child closed in on high school graduation, Missy a black terrier mix with a few splashes of white was adopted from the local animal shelter. Shortly after, Snickers a bouncy grey and white pure bred miniature schnauzer was added to as a companion for Missy. Before long our oldest boy was off to pursue his own dreams and make his own life. Snickers was sassy and playful. She loved being in the yard and going for walks. Missy became the mother hen. Not only was she protective of Snickers but of my wife and I. She had keen instincts for signs of danger. Once when my wife was walking with her on the property, Missy suddenly took a defensive pose. There among the grass and fallen tree limbs was a snake coiled to strike. Missy positioned herself between the large snake and my wife. Stopping a few paces behind Missy, my wife witnessed the dual between the two. Realizing that my wife had stopped, Missy started barking intensely as if ordering her to get to safety. Efforts by my wife to get her to come failed. She was standing her ground, protecting my wife from harm. Like a mongoose and a cobra, they took turns lunging at each other. Once Missy was certain that her owner arrived safely at the patio, Missy ended the dual. Both she and the snake were unharmed. The physical dual had ended in a tie. Missy, however, had gotten the only victory she cared about, the safety of my wife. Of course Missy was well rewarded.

In August 2005, Hurricane Katrina devastated the area. It was also the senior year of our youngest son. The time was growing near when he would leave the nest. By October we moved into the FEMA trailer positioned just off the back door to my in-laws home. After moving what belongings we had left into storage, we settled in to our new 250 square foot travel trailer. We packed our two canine children. Andrew opted for a room in his grandparent's house. The beds in the camper were too small to accommodate his 6 foot frame. Sorry, but the wife and I at 5'2" and 5'8" were not giving up the Queen bed. Within about a week we fenced off a small area for Snickers and Missy to play in. That is when Snickers displayed an unfortunate talent - Escape Artist. She escaped more than a half dozen times (I was beginning to think that even Alcatraz couldn't have held her). Each time we got her back we surveyed the pen for weak spots and reinforced them. Our efforts seemed to be futile as she just kept finding new holes in the fence. It wasn't until we were puppy sitting another dog that we got some insight into Snickers escape methods. Yes, both dogs got out. We repaired the fence again, took about a five minute break for water and let the dogs out to potty. In no time she had nearly ripped through the fencing with her teeth and was starting through the hole when I caught her. The extra strong fencing we had purchased to provide security inside and out was nothing to her jaws. "Snippers" might have been a more appropriate name for Snickers had we only known 16 months earlier.

In January 2006 puppy number three was adopted. She was a smaller schnauzer, black with splashes of white. My wife named her Skittles (the candy names were not lost on us). Most of the time we simply called her "Bit" short for Little Bit. It was during the ride to pick her up that a pattern was repeating itself. Each time a child of ours had either left the nest or were within months of leaving, my wife got a dog. I asked her directly if she was aware the particular pattern of behavior I was inquiring about. She gave me a knowing grin but me to say it: You keep refilling the nest. One kid gone one dog, two kids gone two dogs. Now kid number three was leaving and we were on our way to pick up dog number 3. My wife did not dispute my assessment responding only with agreeable laughter. In this situation I was grateful that we didn't have more kids.

Skittles was our yapper and lap dog. She loved being held. She also our most hyper with a two second attention span. It also turned out that she had a super power, a vertical leap greater than much larger dogs.

After a brief period of helping Skittles and the other dogs

get adjusted to each other, we put them in the outdoor pen together. The issues with our escape artist (Snickers) seemed to be resolved. Placing Skittles over the three foot gate, we watched her interaction with Missy and Snickers. All was well so we went inside for some lunch. About ten minutes later we heard what appeared to be the bark of a puppy. Initially, my wife and I both thought "she sure is loud for a puppy." As Skittles repeated her barking, my wife realized in disbelief, that the bark wasn't loud, it was close. Opening the door slowly, there sat Skittles on the porch of the travel trailer. At less than six inches in height she managed to get over the three foot gate. Not entirely convinced of her leaping ability she was placed back in the pen. We inspected for any possible openings in the fence and gate. Satisfied that the pen was secure, we returned to our lunch. Less than five minutes later, that tiny bark was outside the door again. She did it again, a third time, in full view of our disbelieving eyes. From behind the plywood gate a pair of tiny paws curled themselves over the top. Within the blink of an eye she was on the porch settling quietly and comfortably in my wife's lap.

With the nest fully refilled and our children having started their own lives a new chapter began. As our pups grew so did our family. During the lifetimes of our pups we were blessed with six grandchildren. We took them on trips, spoiled them with toys, outfits, grooming and belly rubs. We gave them lots of love and attention. At times they were fussy and fought like siblings. They each had their own needs and wants. Like our human children they were also loving and loyal. When we became ill or distressed each one stayed by our side until they sensed that we doing better. Only then would they resume their daily routine of eating, playing and sleeping.

Each communicated differently. Missy was the only one with true resounding bark. Snickers "bark" was a bur-r-r or a rue-u-u and Skittles voice reminded me of Dino on the Flintstones. Then there were times when she would sit in front of me, yapping incessantly that she reminded of one those electronic toy dogs from the 1960's (You Baby Boomers know the one I'm talking about). It was white with brown floppy ears, had a cord attached just long enough for someone three feet tall to operate. It did only four things: walked about an inch, sat, yapped then flipped. That was also my Skittles. The one major difference between the toy and Skittles was their battery packs. The toy dog took a single "C" sized battery which lasted about five minutes after which the toy was never played with again. Skittles, on the other hand made the Energizer Bunny look fatigued and slow. As lovable as she was, there were times when I wished I could remove her batteries.

As I sit writing this chapter about refilling the nest, the similarities to own children is mind blowing. Missy, just like child number 1, was the big sister, dominant and caring at the same time. Whenever she sensed a threat to her siblings, she would not hesitate to protect them. On the other hand when they became an annoyance to her she didn't hesitate to project that dominant growl (so to speak). Snickers, like child number two, was the most quiet. We never saw precursors to occasional conflict in her with the other dogs. It would simply go from quiet to very loud, very quickly (as any parent will attest, this is normal between siblings). Snickers also was not one to back away from greater odds and was sneaky fast. We observed the latter one evening after work. Some of the neighbors chickens found their way into our yard. Before we realized it Snickers had a mouthful of chicken feathers. Amazingly, the chicken escaped unharmed. Snickers also enjoyed being outdoors but welcomed a warm, comfortable bed at the end of the day. Finally we have Skittles. In my mind she was most like her human predecessor, child number three. As mentioned earlier, Skittles was our acrobat with amazing leaping abilities and was often outspoken (or is it out-yapped?). There were times when Skittles would make a mess and immediately seek us out. She would sit in front of us with that tiny, innocent guilt-ridden face. Then with a combination of yap and whine she seemed to plead her case. Translation "I didn't do it", or "if I did it at all, I only did it a little." These are only a few snippets of those similarities. That trio of Missy, Snickers and Skittles had long canine lives (15 years, 17 years/10 months and 13 years).

With the passing of Missy and Skittles, Snickers was without a playmate. For the first time in her life she was alone. The yard she loved no longer seemed to interest her. A heavy sadness was apparent in her body language. Though she responded well to our attention, it simply wasn't enough. Something had to done. In October 2018 we adopted Josephine, a four year old terrier/schnauzer mix, to be her companion. Despite her greatly advanced age Snickers responded well to her new companion. She returned to her beloved yard and there was clearly more bounce in her. Snickers passed away two years later,

beating the average life expectancy for her breed by nearly five years.

Having learned from our experience with Snickers, we were off to the animal shelter. We chose Maggie, a 12 week old, tan and white shitzu/yorkie mix as Josephine's new companion. Josephine has the combined personalities of Missy and Snickers, while Maggie is completely like Skittles. Josephine has a very calm demeanor and loves to go for rides. She is the calming presence I need during the day as Parkinson's continues to progress. Maggie is energetic, demanding and playful. I am her true playmate. She is reminder to me that it's still okay to have fun. As an added bonus, Maggie has become receptive to the lucid dreams I sometimes have or any other distress in she may sense. Whenever she senses any distress she will make every effort to wake me. If I don't respond, she will try to wake my wife. She does this without having any special training.

The naysayers who may argue that no animal can ever replace a child, will find no disagreement in me. Children fill a far more precious place in our hearts and souls. Raising a child to be productive, responsible, law abiding adults requires great dedication and love from their parents. In turn most of us will get to relive the childhoods of our children through our grandchildren. As for our pets, they fill that physical void left by our children. They allow us to continue to brush up on our care giving and nurturing skills. For me, it is a reminder that silence is sometimes silver. What's golden are the sounds of little beating hearts and the pitter-patter of tiny paws. Their physical presence, in turn helps to trigger memories of a time when five (or, at times, six or seven) wasn't a crowd and our home was filled with the sounds of our children.

Part II

Vehicles of Influence:

The Old Red Truck

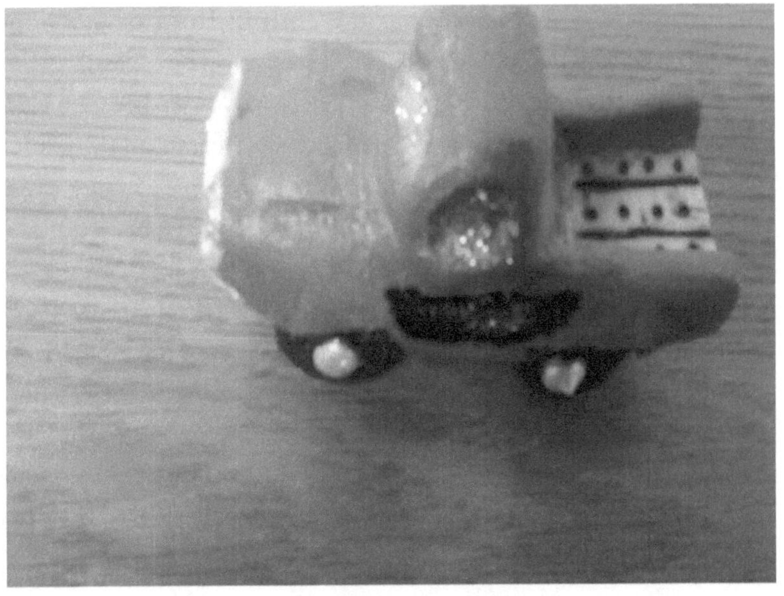

CARVING OF BROTHER Chris' Red Truck with it's original wooden bed

It wasn't much to look at when my brother brought it home. On the outside the red paint had faded to primer on some areas and primer to rust in others. In the bed of the truck were a few wooden planks and it's ability to carry any cargo long passed. Inside the original brown upholstery on the bench seat was dry and falling apart. On the driver's side floorboard holes had rusted through and asphalt from the street below was visible. But, there it was parked on the curb in front of our house, a 1953 Chevrolet pickup truck. It's new owner wasn't even old enough to drive. The year was 1967. My older brother was just 14 years old according to his birth certificate anyway. He was a young teen by modern standards but a man in my eyes. Six years separated us in age but it easily could have been 20. He had experienced tough times and had a survivor's instinct.

Having learned the value of hard work at an early age he peddled a bike miles to deliver newspapers and washed cars at our dad's used car business to earn extra money. My father was meticulous about everything he did. He also had a gift for assessing cars and other things for their monetary value which seemed to be lost by their original owners. This talent was passed on to my brother.

The old red truck, a castaway of rust and bolts was valueless to it's previous owners. In their minds, perhaps, it's usefulness was long gone. However, that 14 year old saw the hidden potential in that bucket of bolts. In a short period of time he transformed it into a thing of beauty. A new coat of paint, new sturdy steel bed on the outside, new floor-boards and black upholstery on the inside.

While the emerging young man saw the value of his investment, the boy inside allowed him to have fun with it. He loved showing it off and taking us for rides. The best part for me was when he sat me in his lap on the driver's side, teaching me where the starter was (on the floor for that model), the gear shift, wiper switch and of course that great big steering wheel. He started by first letting me steer it. Next came the tricky part, learning how to shift correctly as he operated the clutch, brakes and accelerator. He was a very patient teacher especially when he heard that unpleasant grinding sound indicating I missed the correct gear. He never got mad. He calmly helped correct my error. His patience brought me great comfort. He literally had my back. Those traits were put into use again when I was in my twenties. I tried and flunked out of college my first attempt.

I thought my dream of earning a college degree was lost. My confidence was severely shaken (an early sign of rust buildup in my psyche). I was suddenly willing to work at jobs I either lacked the talent or the motivation for (mentally, I wasn't hitting my own gears correctly). My big brother would have none of it. Just like years before in that old red truck, he had my back. He assessed accurately, that the key to success lay in the halls of academia, not on construction sites. He wasn't going to let his little brother rust away and keep grinding the gears. After "conspiring" with our mother to get me back into college, he sent me on my way. The renovation had begun. In time I would earn a Master's Degree, get married and help raise three great kids. The renovation was now complete. Fifty-three years have now passed. That old red truck is long gone but the memories and lessons I learned continue to live on.

The SS Chum

(A True Fish Feeding Adventure)

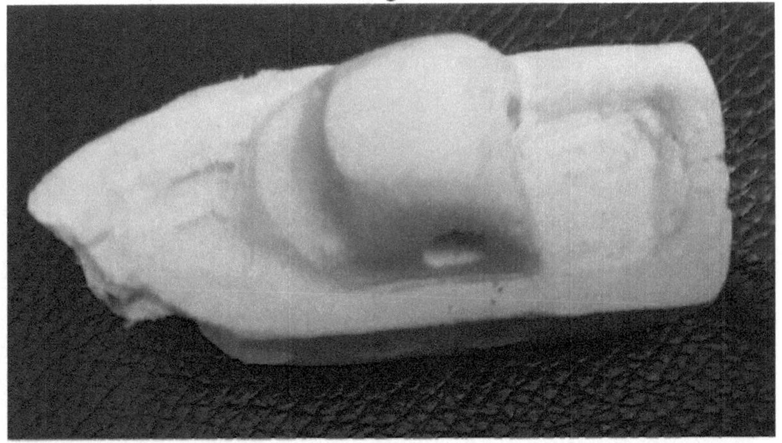

THE SS CHUM AS SEEN through the eyes of our crew before leaving dock See the after photo at the end of the story)

Chumming: 1. To be friendly with someone, to pal around with, 2. Use of bait consisting of a mix of fish, bone and blood or any smelly concoction that is thrown into the water to attract fish. Both definitions apply to this story.

MANY YEARS AGO GIACOMO (thats me), joined bunch of his paisanos Vito, Biagio, Luigi, Giuseppe, Giovanni, Pasquale, Guido and Fosco for a deep sea fishing trip in the Gulf of Mexico. We agreed to spend the night at Vito's house in Mississippi on Friday so that we would be on time for the Charter on Saturday. My thought was to get some good sleep and be well rested for a long day of fishing. I also understood that Fosco and Luigi may have different ideas. Not that straight as an arrow Vito was completely innocent as he made sure they knew where to find the shaving cream. I grew up with these guys and experienced my share of Barbasol bombs, melon missiles and black pepper pingers just to name a few (my family's precursor to paint ball wars). And, although I may not have started any of those previous mealy skirmishes, I like to think I gave as good as I got. That made growing up with them fun. However, having never been deep sea fishing before, I wanted to make the most of this opportunity. Besides there was only one bathroom and I didn't want to spend sleep time with clean-up time.

After getting settled in, we went to a local restaurant to eat. Taking our time, we were entertained by the comedians in the group Luigi, Giovani and Fosco. Bellies full and the time nearing 11:00 pm we returned to the house for an interesting night ahead. I grabbed a spot on the floor and wrapped myself as tightly as I could in a blanket head to foot. I was well prepared for the practical joke goblin, Luigi. My ears locked in on the subtle shuffle of his feet as he made his rounds to his unsuspecting victims, shaving cream in hand. Finally, he turned his attention to me. Certain I was sound asleep, he began tugging at the blanket trying to find an opening in my defense. Several attempts were made, each with increased intensity. Each without success. Conceding defeat, I overheard Luigi tell a fellow conspirator as he laughed, "I think he welded himself in that thing." Now able to let my guard down, I fell asleep. What went on the rest of the night I cannot tell you. I know who ever was still awake was having a good time. They were just a bunch of guys chumming around, pulling pranks and telling jokes.

On Saturday morning about 5:30 a.m. everyone began to wake up. I felt well rested and ready to do some fishing. Although, I had never been on a charter boat, I had no concerns about sea sickness. While in the Marine Corps I served on two Navy ships in high seas without incident. That would not change this day.

As time was growing increasingly short, we loaded up the cars with sandwiches, snacks and people. We swung by a drive through for some breakfast on the go. Arriving at the marina about 30 minutes early our party was given the go ahead to board. As we began loading our stuff everything was going fine that is until the now infamous sandwich incident. Stepping on board the boat it suddenly shifted. As I tried to regain my balance my arms jerked upward tossing half the sandwiches overboard.

TIME STOPPED, JAWS DROPPED, PUPILS DILATED, FACES TURNED RED AND...THE EARTH STOPPED ROTATING.

It was as if our group were witnessing the end of the world. I suppose the prospect of six hours at sea with little to eat may feel that way to some. Anyhow, after Biagio and others completed their commentary on my clumsiness and momentary loss of intellect (feel free to fill in what you think was actually said), our party boarded and settled in. The captain then set a course for our fishing destination.

It took about an hour to reach the place where our captain assured us there would be fish. Those that stayed up all night used the hour to catch up on some sleep. Giuseppe, Guido and I were well rested and chose too stay up top and enjoy the fresh air.

As the engines slowed, the captain announced it was time to fish. The water was relatively calm early on which made it easy to relax. Responding to the captain's call Vito, Biagio and Luigi found their way to the aft of the boat in anticipation of getting in their share of fishing. This, however, was short lived as the Gulf waters became increasingly unstable. Within minutes all that positive energy would be replaced with looks of distress as their faces turned odd colors of flushed pink, gray and green. As their chests heaved upward a bit, they clenched their jaws and tightened their lips in an attempt to calm that internal distress. Miraculously it seemed to work. The color was returning. IF ONLY the Gulf's waves had settled down for just ten or twenty minutes they may have been fine. Unfortunately, this was not to be. The high rolling waves proved too much AND... the odd colors returned to their faces as their chests began to heave again. Their internal defenses were failing. Then the final stage: the sea legged shuffle to the sides and back of the boat.

Let the chumming begin!!!!

They would soon be joined in their distress by Pasquale and Giovani. Over the next two hours those five took turns "feeding" the sea life in the deep waters of the Gulf of Mexico. With a mix of Friday's supper and Satuday morning's breakfast, plus any snacks they consumed during the night, they provided the sea life a turbulant smorgasbord of delights.

Then, there were those loose doors at the entrance to the cabin to add injury to insult. It was as if they were controlled by a practical joking ghost grabbing the unsuspecting victim and flinging them headlong to the bottom step. Going through those doors and down the steep stairs was difficult enough on steady legs but on rubbery, sea sick legs (you get the picture). Now some actual fishing did occur as nearly all, if not all was done by three well rested guys. Total fish caught was roughly 12. I caught about three with Giuseppe and Guido catching the other nine. Not great for three hours of fishing. (On the other hand, if I'm a fish why get hooked when there was a whole buffet being delivered to me by Charter boat).

After being cabin bound with five others most of the trip Vito had enough. With the catch rate down to zero (and the fish pretty well fed) the captain was instructed to head back to the marina. Our day at sea was over.

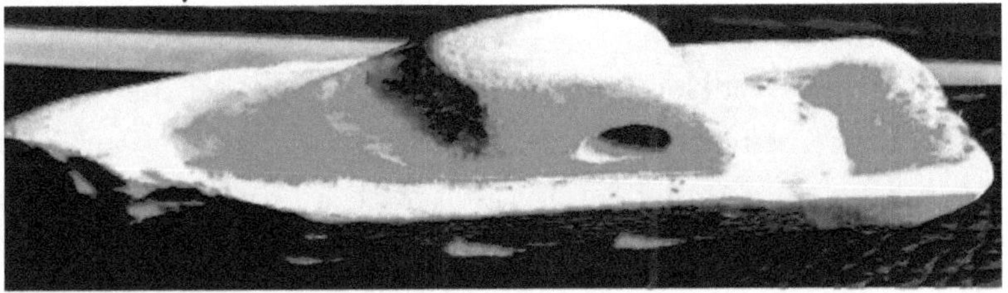

How the Fishing boat may have looked to those who were sea sick

Epilogue

Back at the marina the group agreed that Guido and Giuseppe would divide the day'`s catch between them including my three. I doubt the rest had much of an appetite for anything after their ordeal. Hey, I was okay with it. Giuseppe and Guido did catch most of the fish.

On the front end of the excursion, the sea life at the marina got our lunch. My fault. However, out at sea, most of the rest of our crew fed it much more.

In the end everyone had a good time. Some simply chose to have their fun the night before. And none of us really left empty handed. We all came away with good memories of that single 24 hour period.

Now we all have one of those great memories that starts with "Hey, remember that time, years ago when we all went deep sea fishing" and someone else adds with a grin, "Yeah, you mean when Giacomo dumped all of the sandwiches overboard,,,"

Coming Of Age

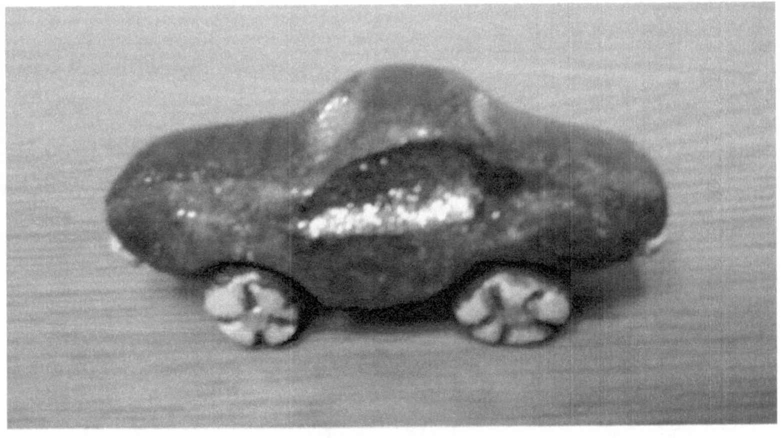

CARVING OF MY SON'S Black Sports Car

Since boyhood my son wanted to be a mechanic. Now his mind was moving in a different direction. Next stop Ole Miss. He has decided to be a mechanical engineer. After all the hugs and well wishing was completed, he got into his car and started the engine. At that very moment the song Born To Be Wild by the band Steppenwolf came on over the house radio:

"Get your motor running.

Head out on the highway, Lookin for adventure..."

How appropriate for the moment. A young man was taking his first step into the unknown. After one successful semester he returned home. He reset his sights on his childhood dream of being a mechanic on the professional racing circuit. Within months he was off again, his destination, technical school in North Carolina to study his chosen profession.

He completed his training successfully, finishing second in his class. After much sacrifice and taking full advantage of every opportunity presented to him, he reached his goal of working in NASCAR.

Over the last 12 plus years he has worked for some of the top owners and drivers. He is now married with two daughters ages 2 years old and the other two months old (our 7th grandchild).

With a successful career in NASCAR established, his greatest adventure is only beginning to evolve: Fatherhood.

Keep your motor running....

BeforeTheir Dreams Were Real

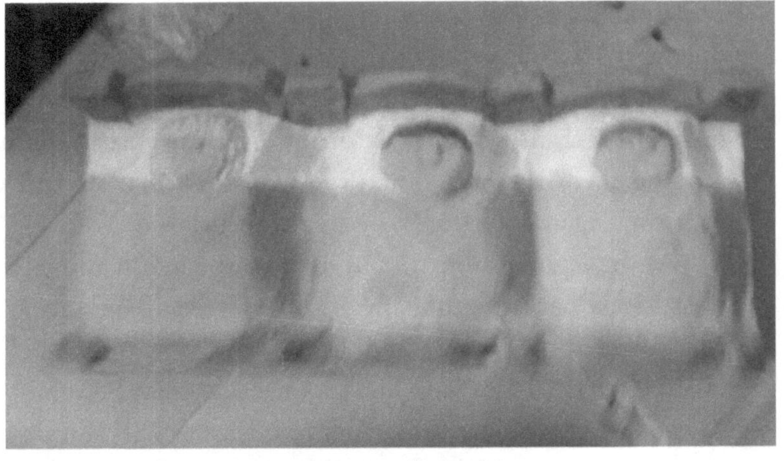

"Before Their Dreams Were Real" Wood Carving

NEARLY ALL ASPIRATIONS begin with childhood dreams. Both my parents come from humble beginnings. My mother dreamed of having a big family. She has six children (I am number 4). My father dreamed of rising above the poverty he was born into. Although, he only completed the 5th grade, he owned several businesses in his lifetime. My father pushed the principle of hard workwhile my mother stressed education. Both principles as well historical events of the time helped my own dreams to evolve.

By the late 1960s the American space program had progressed from sending astronauts into low earth orbit to sending them to the moon. This where my first dreams of a vocation began. I wanted to be an astronaut!

As the Apollo program put men on the moon and brought them safely back the thought of someday being on a rocket to Mars entered my young mind. In time my dreams changed and evolved into real life goals. I had come back to earth, so to speak. My goals as a teenager turned out to be just as lofty. I wanted to go to college either to be a journalist or counselor. As high school graduation neared I was struck by the desire to serve my country and joined the armed forces. In time I did go to college both a Bachelors and Master's Degree. I got married and helped raise three great kids.

Looking back I remembered that as children they had dreams of their own. The oldest wanted to be a teacher, the middle child, a mechanic on a racing team and the youngest was interested in electronics. I envisioned them sleeping and dreaming of their future careers (with embellishments of a proud parent).

I could see my daughter dreaming of her role as a school

teacher. Patiently, she would teach her students how to read, spell, do math and a myriad of other things teachers do. I imagined her thinking that she would be the best teacher the world had ever seen. Fellow teachers would come to her for advice. Education professors clamor to pick her talented young brain in order to improve their programs. World leaders will rush to have a photo taken with her. Not bad for her first day on the job.

Next was my oldest son, dreaming of being the world's greatest race car mechanic. So good would he be that the term speed needed to be redefined, daily. His great skill and reputation reaches mythological proportions. One story would circulate how at age three he souped up his tricycle and out ran a train. Other stories would emerge each one elevating his legend to greater heights. Race teams around the world compete to have him on their teams offering the millions just for his advice. Pretty good for a 9 year old.

Finally, my youngest boy, the electronics genius would reduce today's tech giants to prehistoric levels. His innovations will be posted daily in every news medium in every language around the world. His legend would grow with the invention of his clear coat finger nail sound system in a bottle. Stadium sound will be available with a single brush. Be careful not to snap your fingers though as the heightened volume will blow out all the windows in a 10 mile area. It will be available at Fort Knox for the bargain basement price of one million dollars per once. Better hurry though as only 2000 units were made and orders are pouring in. Then I notice a big grin flash across his face as he realizes that at age 7 he is the world's youngest self made billionaire.

Soon they will all wake up to carry on their daily lives as regular kids. However, their dreams will remain. The day will end. They will close their eyes and revisit that place in twilight where all things are possible. In the passage of time, they all became adults and actually work in the careers they once dreamed about. The embellishments in the story are mine. The hard work and success is theirs.

Today, they all have children of their own. Like their parents they will dare to dream big. I hope so.

Part III

Other Forms of Inspiration

The Grin

FOR MY BROTHER, KEVIN, Thanks for the laughter

At the time I carved the "Grin" it started out as a simple exercise to see what I could do with a wooden ball. When I got tired of the awkwardness of it I painted the few features and declared it finished. It was put on shelf with other pieces with no after thought. However, each time I completed something new that toothy grin was there to greet me. I found myself chuckling at times. It brought an unexpected sense of joy. Before long I realized that there was only one person in my life that ever had that kind of effect on me, my younger brother, Kevin.

Growing up he was sometimes our entertainment. He had a natural gift of humor that was second to none. His often spontaneous shenanigans kept us guessing. That same impulsive humor would give my mother fits when she was trying to correct him. Instead of scolding him, in a mixture of frustration and laughter she would exclaim, "Son, would you knock it off. I'm mad at you!" Then forget what she was mad at him for, "but whatever it was don't do it again." Before long, I noticed that whenever he was up to something he would flash that big toothy grin of his. What he was going to do or say was still unpredictable. My belly and jaw would tighten as I tried to hold back my laughter until his deed was done. As much of a pain as he could be at times, he more than made up for it with his gift of humor. I hope everyone has someone like him in there lives where laughter is only a grin away.

How A Chef Became an Owl

(When the Wood Has a Different Idea)

IIsabel's Night Owl. Still well cared for after more than 10 years

TEN YEARS AGO I DECIDED I was going to surprise my father by doing a carving just for him. He was a great cook my entire life. He was a retired restauranteur at that point with my stepbrother had taken over the day-to-day management of the business. I wanted to carve a chef for him. Going into my shop I carefully selected a block that fit my criteria for the project. I was certain that this block had a chef in it. Carefully, using a pencil, I drew the outline of the chef's hat, face, eyes, arms and legs.

Using my best carving blades I began working toward my desired outcome. Over days and weeks the the body was taking shape. I was on a roll. Then came the "wall". The chef's hat wasn't taking shape. The facial features looked strange. The nose looked like a beak, the arms more like wings. A friend I showed it to thought it looked like an owl. An owl was not what I had in mind. The wood, it seemed, had other ideas. To my disappointment there was no chef in this block. With renewed focus I added more details to the nocturnal bird. After the blade work was complete I needed a paint scheme for the final touches. For reasons, I can't explain, my imagination ran wild. Blue pajamas became a night sky with stars on his cap and body and shooting stars on

his feet. Finally, there he stood in pajamas with eyes closed, seemingly sleep walking. With both feelings of relief and disappointment, I put it away on a shelf with the other carvings. My "chef" had a recipient in mind, my night owl didn't. That changed as my second granddaughter's birthday approached, my wife suggested giving it to her as a gift. Years have gone by now. The little chef has never been carved. My granddaughter is a pre-teen now. I had forgotten about the little owl. That was until she brought it out one day. It was well cared for and cherished.

Looking back that little Night Owl was the best mistake I ever made.

THE LAST EMBRACE

To Uncle Johnny, Manny, Keith, Kevin, Eddie, and all veterans "Thank you for your service"

Completed Memorial Day 2015

A PARENT'S FIRST ACT when their children are born is a gentle embrace and kiss as their first act of love (Hello, welcome home). As they grow this will also be the final act of love (GoodNight) at the end of each day. The cycle will be repeated nearly everyday until the children gradually begin to make their way into world. An embrace for the child during this time tells them that they are safe and protected. For parents an embrace is, not only a sign of love and security, it is also an inspection of their child for signs of injury, distress or happiness (mothers especially can tell if anything is out of place). At bedtime an embrace and a kiss gives assurance to them that they have

made it through the trials and joys of another day. This cycle will continue for a lifetime. As children become adults and leave the nest embraces are given in prayers, letters and unspoken sentiments. They leave with sense a security,a certain set of values and feelings of indestructibility. This is especially true of those who choose to serve in the armed forces. Their child has answered to a higher calling of service to their country. For those families embraces of hello and goodbye have greater importance. It isn't because those acts in childhood were less meaningful. It's just that there is greater uncertainty. Every hello and goodbye may be the last. Those feelings are often unspoken but they are powerful. Each goodbye is given with both fear and hope.

With every hello comes relief, release and guarded happiness.

Most of our veterans will leave the military and live quietly in society. Some will deal with debilitating wounds for the rest of their lives. Others will lose their lives in battle. With their last breath they have given their last of everything: their last ounce of courage, last hellos and last goodbyes...

For the families of the fallen the final embrace comes when the burial flag of the United States, tightly folded into a triangle, is placed in the hands of a parent, spouse or child.

Background Notes

IN JULY 1977 AND FRESH out of high school, I came home and proudly announced to my mother that I had enlisted in the Marines. Her reaction caught me a little off guard. She turned pale and stated "I know you'll go off to war and I'll never see you again." She was expressing a mother's fear. She dodged three bullets when my three oldest brothers were not drafted to serve in Vietnam. She didn't believe, at the time of my announcement, that her luck would hold up. A month later, as we said our goodbyes at the airport, that initial shock seemed to pass. However, when she embraced me, it was different. It was as if she wanted to give a lifetime's worth of a parent's love in that single moment. The fear wasn't gone.

Now, jumping to May of 2015, as Memorial Day was approaching, I had this overwhelming need to do something to honor our fallen service members. I really wanted to do something original. However, after some research looking at hundreds of veterans memorials, I decided on a design which will look familiar to many.

In my version I added the hands receiving the American flag. This element represents and honors the families of those who made the ultimate sacrifice for our great nation. It is one the most meaningful projects I've ever done.

Angels All Around

EIGHTEEN YEARS AGO I began making Christmas ornaments for my wife. I began with clay. About six years later I transitioned to wood carving when my hands became too arthritic to work the clay. I made the usual holiday fare such as snowmen, Santas and even angels. More than 10 years had gone by that I made my last clay angels. Like all the other decorations they owere wrapped up and put away, all but forgotten, until Christmas rolled around again. By the time my children became adults I was solely into wood carving and was making extra sets for them and their children. The set for the grandchildren are put in a curio cabinet where I have access to them anytime.

In 2016 I carved my first set of angels. I wanted these angels to be unique. I wanted them to be more than just about the Christmas season. When the project was completed the number of angels was about 20. I had angels all around me.

As a child I was told that I had a guardian angel. I grew up with images of angels in human form with wings hovering over us. According to the teaching in my own faith, they are assigned to us at conception and remain with us throughout our lives. We have only one (in rare cases two). They are there to protect, guide and pray for us. They do not interfere with free will. As I got older I came to believe that mine was working overtime.

The earliest intervention by my guardian angel occurred was when I was three years old. father, aunts and uncles and my paternal grandparents pitched in and rented a camp on Lake Pontchartrain in the summer of 1962. My mom stayed home with my sister who was only five months old and my younger brother, only a year old the time. My father took my three older brothers and I to the camp. As it was told to me when I was older, the water in the lake was up to the pier due to a storm in the Gulf.

The main activities were swimming, crabbing and fishing. It was the latter that my guardian angel got involved. My father sat me on the railing but holding me tight with both hands. My older brother Chris, who was only nine at the time, was fishing next to us as our

grandfather looked on. As I sat quietly, secure in my father's grasp Chris reeled in a catfish. He then pulled the fish over the pier for grandpa to take the hook out. Seeing the creature my brother had on his fishing line, I got excited and lunged at it. In that moment of excitement, I broke the security of my father's hands and tumbled in the deep, dark waters of the lake. Immediately, my father jumped in. Repeatedly, he push himself below the surface in a determined effort to save his three year old son. One time, two times he came to the surface without me; then down and back up a third time still nothing. Even with high levels of adrenaline pumping through his veins, his body growing tired with each effort. After surfacing from the third attempt, thoughts of finding me alive were beginning to fade for everyone at the camp. Growing weaker but still determined, he forced himself below the surface a fourth time and resurfaced again empty handed. Hope was running on fumes at that point. Even though he was only 27 years old, Dad's fatigue was also likely at a critical level. Whatever he had left, he used for a fifth time. Time, I was told, seemed to stand still during the ordeal. No one knows how long I was under. Likely only minutes. I'm certain few believed I would be found at all. As Chris recalled recently, "If

dad surfaces a fifth time without you, you would have been lost to us.". The fifth time proved to be a charm. My father finally found me near the sandy bottom holding on to one of the pier's pilings. It's still baffling to Chris today. "What kid does that, grabs

on to something in a situation like that." Anyhow, after getting me back on dry land no resuscitation was needed. As Chris noted, "you started crying then started running around like a normal kid, thank goodness"

For me, I have no doubt that it was my guardian angel who protected me. He wrapped my little arms around that piling to keep the tide from taking me beyond my father's search area to a watery grave. He then provided a barrier that protected me and kept me from ingesting any water. Those actions gave my father enough time to find me alive.

Other incidents in which my guardian angel was involved:

Fall of 1966 - Hit by an automobile and knocked unconscious. Suffered nose bleeds for years after. 1975- fell face first onto a "cheese-grater" asphalt parking lot ripping a hole in my face below my right eye exposing my cheek bone. Hospitalized two weeks and required reconstructive surgery to repair the hole in my face. I also suffered a concussion and swelling on the entire right side of my body. The doctor said it a miracle that I didn't lose my right eye. To add insult to injury I missed a month of school and only had ten days to make it up or fail the year. My math teacher didn't think I could make it up in time. It took an order from the assistant principal to get the assigned makeup work in that class. I must admit, my math teacher was correct - I did not turn in the required make up work in 10 days. I was 7 days off. It took only 72 hours (pulling all nighters for 3 days) to complete the make up work in five of my six classes (I got a pass from my Physical Education teacher). The following school year I crammed 2 years of studies into one and graduated in just three years (That guardian angel got pushy at times).

Another clear act of guardian angel involvement came one evening in late 1994. I was driving home on a nearly 24 mile stretch of bridge all over water. Traveling southbound from my job on the north shore I fell asleep behind the wheel at mile marker 11 and awakened 5 miles later at mile marker 16. The shock of what had transpired kept me awake until I arrived home another 20 miles away. During that five mile stretch, I somehow managed not to drift into the other lane or hit the guard rail. This was not a case of simply being distracted and losing track of the miles. I was stone cold asleep for five miles of open flat bridge (which does run in a perfect straight line) over 23 plus miles of open water. No doubt.

Each of those incidents the impacts were only fractions away from being life threatening. There were many other incidents in which my spiritual protector intervened and kept me on my life's path. From my early 20s to the present I have crossed paths with people with angel-like qualities. They possessed extraordinary insight, wisdom, discipline, compassion and toughness. Some helped raise me but have since passed away. Others continue to be present in my life providing comfort, care and spiritual guidance. They also gave me a good kick in the pants whenever I needed it. Some came in the form of friends who called when I least expected with words of encouragement. Later in my career, there was a coworker who was always the first to console me when my parents died and when my wife was seriously ill. On occasion they would appear as a strangers, people who's name I never got but somehow the rest of my day seemed better for having crossed their path. They came in many shapes, sizes, colors and ages. Through the years they all made my life a little better.

Throughout my life I repeatedly beat the odds. In primary school, my grades were very average and I wasn't considered college material. At least according to my high school counselor. At the time I was being told this by someone I respected, there was that inner supernatural voice inside my head that told me differently. It took longer than I planned but in 1992 I earned my Bachelor's Degree followed by a Master's Degree in 1994. During this period my heavenly protector provided that spiritual whisper that cut through and negated my self doubt. I also came to realize that I have benefited from the guardian angels of others. In early 1995 I was bringing my date home around 11 pm. The next thing I recall was my steering wheel being pulled hard to the right and a frantic voice yelling words that my brain could not immediately register. Once I was fully conscious from another unplanned mini-nap, my date revealed to me in very disbelieving tone, that I had fallen asleep behind the wheel. The car was drifting toward the shiny belly of a tanker truck. Our lives were spared. As to my date. I delivered to her home safely, if shaken. Of course one can only guess how that relationship turned out... It was our first date. Happily, she became my wife 15 months later.

FINALLY, IN SEPTEMBER 2016

I was diagnosed with Parkinson's Disease. I worked with some good, conscientious people. They responded to their angel's guidance on my behalf. As a result I was able to stretch my career three more years until my retirement in September

2019. There is no way I could have made it that far without the interventions of all those angels.

In the process of writing this piece, I imagined my guardian angel being in distress at times, having to watch out for this extraordinarily clumsy human being. During particularly challenging times in my life, I could see him looking at his watch and tapping his feet, hoping someone would come by and give him a break. I could hear him thinking (in my formative years), "I sure hope his mother isn't running late."Later, it was and perhaps still is, "I sure hope his wife isn't running late.". My sister, Jackie disagrees with me on this last part. "The Devil has tried to kill you too many times for you to have only one guardian angel." The way she sees it, I have at least three. However, I believe I have one extra-ordinary guardian angel assigned to me. Then there are those good people who live in God's grace, are receptive to the guidance of their guardian angels and act for the good of others. It happens everyday all around us if we only pay attention. I am living proof.

Part IV

WOODSHED HOUSEKEEPING

THE SS CHUM: Shortly after photos were taken of the SS Chum for the book she sustained damage in a non-maritime incident. It occurred when the author's youngest pup mistook it for a chew toy. Damage resulted in the production of 6 tooth picks and a slobbered exterior.

None of the passengers on the SS Chum had real italian first names. Exercisng creative license and a little research , I added Italian pseudonymns to honor my Sicilian heritage. My paternal grandfather is from Siracusa, Sicily.

Wood Carvings:

ALL OF THE WORK WAS done by my hands including the painting. I have the scars on my fingers to prove it. Yes, I do use a carving glove. Unfortunately, like dog toys, they are not indestructable.

My planned progression of my wood carving hobby (Chain Saw sculpting) has been has been eliminated due to Parkinson's progression. A knick from a carving knife is one thing, but one from a chainsaw? Not a very pleasant picture. So there will be no future stories using this medium. On the other hand hammer and chisel is not out of the question.One log sculpture completed, about 19 more to go. Look for that issue in about 40 years.

Final Notes

AS I WAS LOOKING THROUGH photos for the book, it dawned on me that a few things were unintentionally left out. So if sales are twice the number of my immediate family (I come from a big family) there could be an update down the road.

It is December 23, 2020. It is quiet and a slight chill fills the kitchen air. Christmas is just two days away. The ornaments I carved for 2020 will soon find their way to the hands of my children. I have also added to my wife's Santa Clause collection. I carve one or two for her each year. I try very hard to make each one unique. My best guess is that she has 20 or more ranging from hanging ornaments to table ornaments. The ones over the last two years seem to have some of my mannerisms. So for better or worse she has reminders of me laying around.

With that I leave you with a carving of a trait that many in my family say I do best.

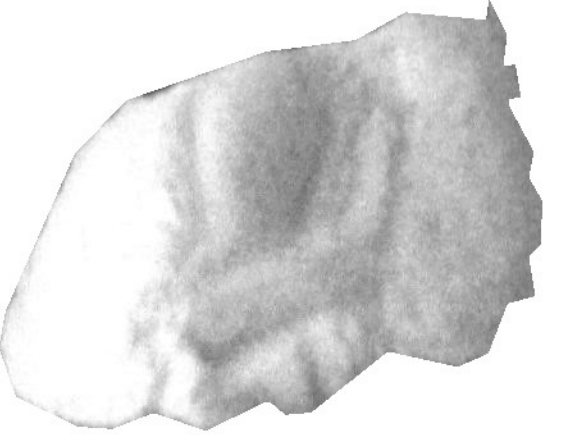

About the Author

Retired. Happily Married to my fantastic wife, Suzannne (25 years come this spring) 3 children, 7 grandchildren. Marine Corps veteran. Diagnosed with Parkinson's Disease in late 2016. I now spend my time writing, wood crafts and tending to my vegetable garden. Additionally, I have two very spoiled pups to keep happy. This is my first book.

About the Publisher

Stories written from the heart and chiseled into memory